D1443806

A Robbie Reader

# Charles Schulz

## THE STORY OF THE PEANUTS GANG

by
Barbara Marvis

P.O. Box 196
Hockessin, Delaware 19707
Visit us on the web: www.mitchelllane.com
Comments? email us: mitchelllane@mitchelllane.com

Printing      2      3      4      5      6      7      8      9

## A Robbie Reader

| | | |
|---|---|---|
| Hilary Duff | Dale Earnhardt, Jr. | Thomas Edison |
| Albert Einstein | Philo T. Farnsworth | Harley-Davidson |
| Henry Ford | Robert Goddard | Johnny Gruelle |
| Mia Hamm | Tony Hawk | Syd Hoff |
| LeBron James | Donovan McNabb | Shaquille O'Neal |
| Barbara Park | Alex Rodriguez | Dr. Seuss |
| **Charles Schulz** | Jamie Lynn Spears | |

Library of Congress Cataloging-in-Publication Data
Marvis, Barbara J.
    Charles Schulz: the story of the Peanuts gang / by Barbara Marvis.
        p. cm.—(A Robbie reader)
    Summary: A biography of the creator of the popular "Peanuts" comic strip. Includes bibliographical references and index.
        ISBN 1-58415-289-3 (library bound)
    1. Schulz, Charles M.—Juvenile literature. 2. Cartoonists—United States—Biography—Juvenile literature. I. Title. II. Series
PN6727.S3 Z77 2005
741.5'092—dc22
[B]                                                                  2004009308

**ABOUT THE AUTHOR:** Barbara Marvis is the author of more than twenty books for children and young adults. With an M.Ed. in remedial reading, Ms. Marvis specializes in stories for beginning readers and nonfiction for middle-grade at-risk readers.

**PHOTO CREDITS:** Cover: Shooting Star; p. 4 Getty Images; p. 6 Bill Melendez; p. 8 Corbis; p. 10 Reuters NewMedia Inc./Corbis; p. 12 AP Photo; p. 14 Shooting Star; p. 16 Getty Images; p. 18 Corbis; p. 20 Shooting Star; p. 22 top and bottom, Corbis; p. 24 Amagen; p. 26 Bill Melendez; p. 28 Bill Melendez.

# TABLE OF CONTENTS

**Chapter One**
**A Big Risk** ............................................................ 5

**Chapter Two**
**A Boy Named Sparky** ...................................... 9

**Chapter Three**
**Hard Times** ....................................................... 13

**Chapter Four**
**United Feature Syndicate** ............................. 17

**Chapter Five**
**The Little Red-Haired Girl** ........................... 21

**Chapter Six**
**Good-bye Good Ol' Charlie Brown** ............. 25

**Chronology** ...................................................... 29
**Selected Works** ............................................... 30
**To Find Out More** .......................................... 31
**Glossary** ........................................................... 31
**Index** ................................................................ 32

Charles Schulz is standing in front of a stained glass window that shows his characters Snoopy and Woodstock.

# A BIG RISK

It was a few weeks before Christmas in 1965. Charles Schulz (SHUHLTS) was worried. His comic strip *Peanuts* was going on television. He didn't know if the show would be any good. Or if anyone would watch it. When the idea first came up two years earlier none of the TV networks was interested. What if the show failed?

The *Peanuts* comic strip had been in the newspapers for fifteen years. But Charles Schulz drew the cartoon on paper. The characters did not walk or talk. Maybe fans would be disappointed. What would people think when they saw his cartoons move?

This is Bill Melendez. He is the animator for the *Peanuts* TV specials. He makes the cartoon characters walk and talk.

Schulz did not have much time to make the show. He was given only four months. All the drawings, the script, and the music had to be finished. The crew worked hard and met the deadline.

But then there was another catch. The TV network said the action didn't move fast enough. They didn't like the music, either. They wanted a different laugh track. And time was running out.

When it came time for the show to air, everyone had their fingers crossed. Would anyone watch their show?

*A Charlie Brown Christmas* was a great success. A man named Bill Melendez (Meh-LEN-dez) made the Peanuts gang come to life. He is called an **animator** (AAH-neh-MAY-ter). An animator makes cartoon characters walk and talk. Charles Schulz needn't have worried. Everyone loved the first Charlie Brown special.

Charles Schulz draws Snoopy.

# A BOY NAMED SPARKY

Charles Schulz was born on November 26, 1922 in Minneapolis, Minnesota. His father was Carl Schulz and he was a barber. His mother was Dena Schulz and she was a housewife. Charles was their only child.

When Charles was only two days old, his uncle nicknamed him Sparky. That was short for Sparkplug. Sparkplug was a horse in the comic strip *Barney Google*. The nickname stuck with him all his life.

Soon, Charles and his family moved to St. Paul, Minnesota. By kindergarten, Sparky knew he was born to draw. "The teacher gave us

Charles Schulz was very close to both of his parents. Neither one had any artistic talent, however. After school, Sparky would visit his father at the barber shop. He would wait quietly until his father was done cutting hair. Then he would take a nickel from the cash register to buy a candy bar. Father and son would walk home together, eat dinner with Dena and then read the comic strips in the paper. He always had great memories of his early childhood. Here he stands, many years later, in front of a mural of Snoopy and Woodstock.

huge sheets of white paper and large black crayons. I drew a man shoveling snow," Charles recalled. His teacher liked his artwork. She said, "Someday, Charles, you are going to be an artist."

Sparky remembers he always wanted to make a daily comic strip. Every day, he read the comic strips in the paper with his mom and dad. Then they talked about them.

Sparky also loved sports. When he was growing up, there were no organized sports like Little League or Youth Soccer. So he and his friends would play baseball and hockey in the streets.

By the time Charles reached junior high school, he was the youngest and smallest kid in the class. He didn't believe that anyone liked him. He became very lonely.

Charles had fun with his mom and dad. But when he was away from them, he was quiet and shy.

Charles Schulz based his cartoon strip *Peanuts* on things that happened in his life. Charles had five children who provided him with lots of ideas for his cartoons.

# HARD TIMES

When Sparky went to St. Paul's Central High School, he didn't have many friends. He never asked a girl out on a date. He thought no one would go out with him.

When he was a senior in high school, Charles gave his drawings to the yearbook. The editors didn't use a single piece of his art. He did, however, sell his first cartoon to a newspaper during this time.

Charles loved drawing very much. His mother said he should go to art school. The family worked hard to pay the **tuition** (two-IH-shun) for his art school. Charles only earned a C in his first drawing class.

The *Peanuts* characters that Charles created have become very famous. Here you see some of the characters dressed to play several sports. Charlie Brown loves sports just like Charles Schultz did.

World War II put a stop to his art school. Sparky was drafted into the army in 1943. During his basic training, his mother died. Charles was never hurt in the war. But losing his mother hurt him a lot. He was very sad.

After the war, Sparky got a job as an art instructor. He also sold some cartoons to a magazine called the *Saturday Evening Post*.

He made up a series called *L'il Folks*. The *St. Paul Pioneer Press*, his hometown newspaper, published them every Sunday.

Charles now had a regular job. Each week, he drew a comic strip that was printed in the local newspaper. The *Saturday Evening Post* bought more of his cartoons, too.

Charles felt bold. He went to the editor of the local paper and asked if his cartoon could appear more often. The answer was 'no.' Then he asked for more money. The answer was 'no.'

Charles said, "Perhaps I should just quit drawing it."

The editor said 'yes,' and Charles lost his job.

Charles Schulz was not an instant success with his cartoons. But once his comic strip became well known, he found a lifelong career.

# UNITED FEATURE SYNDICATE

Charles was surprised when he was fired, but he did not give up. He looked for other ways to sell his cartoons.

He began sending them to **syndicates** (sin-dih-KITS). A syndicate is a group who helps cartoonists sell their work to newspapers all over the country. Many newspapers can buy the same artwork. The artist can make more money this way.

In 1950, United Feature Syndicate in New York signed a contract with Sparky. They asked him to make a daily comic strip. It would be based on Sparky's cartoon *L'il Folks*.

During his entire career, Charles drew all his strips by himself. He never had any help.

The syndicate did not like the name *L'il Folks*. There was already a cartoon named *L'il Abner* and one named *Little Folks*. Sparky suggested *Charlie Brown* or *Good Ol' Charlie Brown*. The syndicate did not like either name. They came up with their own name: *Peanuts*.

Sparky didn't like that at all. "No one calls small children 'peanuts.'" he said. Besides, he thought, no one in the strip was named Peanuts. But the syndicate had made up its mind. Because Sparky was a young, unknown cartoonist, he didn't have any say in the matter.

On October 2, 1950, the very first *Peanuts* strip was printed. Seven newspapers carried it. Charles Schulz earned $90 for his first week.

Unlike all the other characters in the *Peanuts* strip, the little red-haired girl never appears in person. Finally, just before the strip ended, Schulz shows her dancing with Snoopy. But she is just a shadow. In real-life, Sparky was in love with a girl named Donna Johnson. She had bright red hair. She married another man and Charles was heartbroken.

# THE LITTLE RED-HAIRED GIRL

The *Peanuts* comic strip started with just four characters: Charlie Brown, Patty, Shermy, and Snoopy. Over the years, other characters were added: Violet, Lucy, Linus, Pig Pen, Franklin, Schroeder, Peppermint Patty, Marcie, and Woodstock.

And the little red-haired girl. Charlie Brown likes the little red-haired girl. But he is too shy to sit next to her or give her a valentine.

Sparky wrote many of the *Peanuts* stories and created characters based on things that happened in his life. In real life, Charles was in love with a woman named Donna Johnson. She

In 1974, Schulz was named Grand Marshal of the Tournament of Roses Parade in Pasadena, California. Above, he is shown riding with his daughter, Amy.

To the right: Charles worked for many years at the same drawing board he bought at the beginning of his career for $23.

had bright red hair. Sparky asked her to marry him. She said 'no.' She married another man and Sparky was heartbroken.

Soon he met Joyce Halverson. Joyce and Sparky were married in April 1951. They had five children. Many ideas for the comic strip came from their children.

When their daughter Meredith was two, they bought her a toy piano. This gave Charles an idea. He drew Schroeder with his toy piano.

Then there was the time at the dinner table. Daughter Amy was being noisy. Charles asked her to be quiet. Amy closed her mouth. She picked up some bread and put butter on it. "Am I buttering too loud for you?" she asked. Charles put those exact words in his strip.

By this time, the family had moved to California. Charles would spend the rest of his life there. But not married to Joyce. In 1972, Joyce and Charles split.

In 1973, Charles married Jeannie Forsyth. He spent the rest of his life with her. They lived at 1 Snoopy Place.

Charles and his second wife, Jeannie.

# GOOD-BYE GOOD OL' CHARLIE BROWN

Charlie Brown, Snoopy, and the rest of the Peanuts gang made Charles Schulz a very rich man. Soon there were Peanuts calendars, datebooks, clothing, and dolls.

Charles was a **generous** (JEN-er-us) man, too. He gave a lot of his money to good causes like the Jean and Charles Schulz Information Center at Sonoma State University.

All his life, Charles worked very hard. He was always working right up to the end. In all the years that Sparky drew the comic strip *Peanuts*, he never had anyone help him. He designed and drew every panel.

In November 1999, Charles Schulz learned that he had cancer. He announced that

In 1996, Charles Schulz earned a star on the Hollywood Walk of Fame. He is shown here in the middle. Bill Melendez, his animator, is to his left.

he would retire. His final daily strip was in January 2000. The final Sunday strip ran one month later on Sunday, February 13. But Charles Schulz had died the night before. All the fans of Charlie Brown and Snoopy were sad. There would not be any new adventures of the Peanuts gang.

Their creator had died. **Tributes** (TRIB-yoots) began to pour in right away. Other cartoonists dedicated their strips to Sparky's memory. The airport near his home was renamed the Charles M. Schulz–Sonoma County Airport. The Baseball Hall of Fame set up an **exhibit** (ig-ZIB-it) in Cooperstown, New York called, "You're in the Hall of Fame, Charlie Brown!" because nearly 2,000 *Peanuts* strips were about baseball.

Charlie Brown lives on, however, in reprints and in dozens of books about the Peanuts gang. Many of the TV specials are on videotape. You can find them at your library.

This is Bill Melendez as a young man. He has been making *Peanuts* cartoons walk and talk for many years.

1922 born on November 26 in St. Paul, Minnesota

1928 begins kindergarten, where a teacher praises his drawing

1936 enters St. Paul Central High School

1937 first published drawing, a sketch of his dog Spike, appears in newspaper feature *Ripley's Believe It or Not!*

1940 graduates from high school

1943 drafted into U.S. Army; mother dies of cancer

1947 begins publishing cartoon called *L'il Folks* in *St. Paul Pioneer Press*

1950 sells *L'il Folks* to United Feature Syndicate, which changes the strip's name to *Peanuts*

1951 marries Joyce Halverson

1952 *Peanuts* begins appearing on Sunday comic pages

1958 Schulz and his family move to Sebastopol, California

1965 *Peanuts* appears on cover of *Time* magazine; TV special *A Charlie Brown Christmas* premieres

1966 Carl Schulz dies while visiting his son in California

1969 Apollo X astronauts carry Charlie Brown into space with them

1972 divorces Joyce Schulz

1973 marries Jeannie Forsyth

1974 named grand marshall of Tournament of Roses Parade in Pasadena, California

1986 inducted into Cartoonist Hall of Fame and receives Golden Brick award for lifetime achievement

1996 receives his own star on the Hollywood Walk of Fame

1999 announces retirement December 14

2000 dies on February 12, the evening before his final Sunday strip appears

*A Boy Named Charlie Brown* (New York: MetroBooks, 2001).

*Being a Dog Is a Full-Time Job* (Kansas City: Andrews and McMeel, 1994).

*Happiness Is a Warm Puppy* (San Francisco: Determined Productions, 1962).

*How Romantic, Charlie Brown* (New York: Ballantine Books, 1984).

*I Told You So, You Blockhead!* (New York: HarperPerennial, 1999).

*I've Been Traded for a Pizza?* (New York: HarperHorizon, 1998).

*It's a Dog's Life, Snoopy* (New York: Ballantine Books, 2001).

*It's Baseball Season, Again!* (New York: HarperHorizon, 1999).

*The Joy of a Peanuts Christmas* (Kansas City: Hallmark Books, 2000).

*Nice Shot, Snoopy!* (New York: Ballantine Books, 1982).

*Peanuts Jubilee: My Life and Art with Charlie Brown and Others* (New York: Holt, Rinehart and Winston, 1975).

*Peanuts Treasury* (New York: MetroBooks, 2000).

*Peanuts: A Golden Celebration* (New York: HarperCollins, 1999).

*Peanuts: The Art of Charles M. Schulz* (New York: Pantheon Books, 2001).

*Who Was That Dog I Saw You With, Charlie Brown?* (New York: Fawcett Crest, 1973).

*You Can't Win Them All, Charlie Brown* (New York: Fawcett Crest, 1972).

*You Don't Look 35, Charlie Brown!* (New York: Holt, Rinehart and Winston, 1985).

*You've Come a Long Way, Snoopy* (New York: Fawcett Crest, 1976).

Klingel, Cynthia and Robert B. Noyed. *Charles Schulz.* (Wonder Books), Mankato: Child's World, 2001.

Whiting, Jim. *Charles Schulz.* (A Real-Life Reader Biography), Newark, DE.: Mitchell Lane Publishers, Inc., 2003.

Woods, Mae. *Charles Schulz.* (Children's Authors), Edina, Minnesota: Abdo, 2001.

# GLOSSARY

**animator**    (AAH-neh-MAY-ter) — an artist who draws cartoon characters in a series of drawings that makes it look like the cartoons move

**exhibit**    (ig-ZIB-it) — a display

**generous**    (JEN-er-us) — to give a lot

**syndicates**    (sin-dih-KITS) — a group of people who represent an artist and help them sell their artwork to many newspapers at the same time.

**tributes**    (TRIB-yoots) — to show respect or appreciation

**tuition**    (two-IH-shun) — money to pay for school

Art Instruction School 13

Charlie Brown 19

Forsyth, Jeannie (second wife) 23

Halverson, Joyce (first wife) 23

Johnson, Donna 21

Melendez, Bill 6, 7

*Saturday Evening Post* 15

Schulz, Carl (father) 9

Schulz, Charles

    art school 13

    birth of 9

    children of 23

    death of 27

    divorce of 23

    early years 9-15

    education of 9-15

    marriages of 23

    nicknamed "Sparky" 9

    parents of 9, 10

    *Peanuts* comic strip

    debuts 19

Schulz, Dena (mother) 9, 15

United Feature Syndicate 17

World War II 15